RAND

Insuring Mobilized Reservists Against Economic Losses

An Overview

David W. Grissmer,
Sheila Nataraj Kirby,
Man-bing Sze, David Adamson

Prepared for the
Office of the Secretary of Defense

**National Defense
Research Institute**

Operation Desert Storm (ODS) was the first large-scale test of the To-tal Force Policy, which was adopted at the beginning of the All Volunteer Force. This policy relied heavily on the Selected Reserve for meeting military contingencies. The Reserve Force played a critical role in ODS, providing approximately 250,000 personnel. These personnel were particularly critical in providing combat support and combat service support functions, such as logistical and medical support for combat operations. However, one problem encountered by reserve personnel during mobilization was the economic losses faced by many of them. These losses resulted from the difference between their civilian and military incomes, loss of civilian benefits, and additional expenses during mobilization. Such losses during a mobilization may affect future recruiting and retention, and therefore readiness, as well as impose hardships on reserve families.

This report summarizes preliminary results from an ongoing study of the economic losses of reservists upon mobilization and explores one option for addressing this problem, namely, the feasibility of offering insurance protection against such losses. This report was prepared at the request of the Assistant Secretary for Reserve Affairs, who was asked by the United States Senate Committee on Appropriations to examine the feasibility of offering insurance to reservists to protect them against economic losses experienced when they are called to active duty.

The results presented here are based on data from two surveys of reserve personnel and a separately published analysis of the issues faced by insurance companies in offering such insurance. The first survey estimates income losses across the entire Reserve Force for any type of mobilization. The second survey of ODS personnel estimates the economic loss suffered during ODS, the number of reservists indicating an interest in insurance protection, and the amount of insurance desired under different premiums. The analysis of institutional arrangements for providing such insurance entailed examining currently available insurance that covers similar types of risk.

This research is being undertaken for both the Assistant Secretary of Defense (Reserve Affairs) and the Assistant Secretary of Defense (Force, Management, and Personnel). The research is being conducted by the Defense Manpower Research Center, part of RAND's National Defense Research Institute, a federally funded research and development center sponsored by the Office of the Secretary of Defense, the Joint Staff, and the defense agencies.

CONTENTS

Preface   iii

Figures   vii

Tables   ix

Summary   xi

Chapter One
  INTRODUCTION   1

Chapter Two
  ECONOMIC LOSSES OF MOBILIZED RESERVISTS   5
  Income Loss Estimates from the *1986 Survey of Reserve
     Forces*   6
  Results on Reserve Income Losses   8
     How Many Reservists Lose Income During
        Mobilization?   8
     How Much Income Do They Lose?   8
     What Are the Characteristics of the Reservists Who Lose
        Income?   14
  Reserve Income Losses During Operation Desert Storm . .   16

Chapter Three
  DEMAND FOR MOBILIZATION INSURANCE   21
  How Many Would Buy Insurance?   21
  How Much Would They Buy?   24
     Officers   24
     Enlisted Personnel   25
     Summary   25

Chapter Four
    OPTIONS FOR OFFERING INSURANCE   27
    Design Criteria for Income-Protection Insurance   27
    Types of Coverage   28
    The Private Sector as Sole Provider   29
    Lessons from Analogous Types of Insurance   30
        Servicemen's Group Life Insurance   31
        Nuclear Accident Insurance   31
        Flood, Riot, and Crime Insurance   32
        U.S.-Owned Property Overseas   32
        Business Interruption Insurance   32
    Possible Government Roles   33
        Government as Sole Provider   34
        Government as Partner   34

Chapter Five
    PRELIMINARY CONCLUSIONS AND ISSUES FOR
    FURTHER RESEARCH   35
    Reserve Income Losses   35
    Reserve Demand for Insurance   36
    Options for Structuring and Providing Reserve
        Insurance   36
    Issues for Further Research   37

Bibliography   41

FIGURES

1. Percentage of Reservists Losing Income upon Mobilization   9
2. Characterizing Income Losses for Officers Losing Income: 12-Month Mobilization   10
3. Percentile Distribution of Annual Family Income Lost for Officers Losing Income: 12-Month Mobilization . .   10
4. Distribution of Percentage of Family Income Lost for Officers Losing Income: 12-Month Mobilization   11
5. Characterizing Income Losses for Enlisted Personnel Losing Income: 12-Month Mobilization   12
6. Percentile Distribution of Annual Family Income Lost for Enlisted Personnel Losing Income: 12-Month Mobilization   12
7. Distribution of Percentage of Family Income Lost for Enlisted Personnel Losing Income: 12-Month Mobilization   13
8. Reserve Income Losses During Operation Desert Storm   17
9. Lost Income and Additional Expenses of Officers in Operation Desert Storm   18
10. Lost Income and Additional Expenses of Enlisted Personnel in Operation Desert Storm   19
11. Percentage Wanting to Buy Insurance at Two Premium Levels   23
12. Amount of Insurance Desired by Officers: Two Premium Levels   24
13. Amount of Insurance Desired by Enlisted Personnel: Two Premium Levels   25

TABLES

1. Which Officers Lose Income? Differences in
   Characteristics 14
2. Which Enlisted Personnel Lose Income? Differences
   in Characteristics 15
3. Insurance Questions on Survey 22

The Total Force Policy, adopted as part of the move to an All Volunteer Force, placed greater reliance on Reserve Forces to meet military contingencies. Operation Desert Storm (ODS) was the first large-scale test of this policy. Approximately 250,000 reservists were mobilized during ODS; these reservists played a critical role, particularly in logistical and medical support missions. However, one problem that surfaced during ODS was that many reservists suffered economic losses during mobilization. These losses occurred because military pay often did not cover the combined loss of civilian pay and the additional expenses incurred by reservists and their families as a result of mobilization. These losses were substantial in cases where reservists had high civilian incomes or where reservists were self-employed. In the latter case, businesses or partnerships often suffered continuing losses after demobilization because of the loss of client good will. These economic losses may not only create hardships for reserve families during a mobilization but could also make future recruiting and retention more difficult.

Insurance against economic losses has been suggested as a possible solution to this problem (Grissmer et al., 1989). After ODS, Congress requested that the Department of Defense (DoD) study the feasibility of insurance coverage to protect reservists against economic losses during mobilization. This report provides preliminary results from an ongoing RAND study that examines the issue of economic losses during mobilization and the options for addressing this problem.

This report will first document the extent of economic losses for reservists to determine if a policy response is required. If the problem affects few reservists and is confined to few military occupations (perhaps physicians and pilots) and economic losses are fairly uniform, then it might be addressed through targeted compensation programs.

However, if the problem is more widespread and is diffused across most military occupations, and the economic losses are highly variable, then military compensation programs are likely to be inefficient because they cannot be confined only to those suffering economic losses and they cannot be targeted effectively to match the highly variable pattern of economic losses.   Since voluntary insurance coverage can effectively target those suffering losses and can vary in amount to match economic loss patterns, this option is a leading candidate if the problem is widespread and variable in amount.

Since the data show that the problem is not confined to a particular group of reservists, and that economic losses are highly variable, we assess reservists' interest in purchasing such insurance and some government and private-sector roles in providing such insurance. Specifically, the report addresses four issues:

1. What is the extent of income losses for all reservists if mobilized?

2. How frequent and how severe were economic losses during ODS?

3. How many reservists would buy insurance if it were offered and how much would they buy?

4. What roles might government and private-sector carriers play in providing such insurance?

DATA AND APPROACH

We relied on two data sources: the *1986 Survey of Reserve Forces*, consisting of a large, representative sample of reservists who were asked detailed questions regarding civilian and military income; and the *1991 Survey of Mobilized and Nonmobilized Reservists*, which oversampled those in the medical occupational specialties.

From the 1986 data, we estimated income loss by comparing family income with military income in a 12-month mobilization. We assumed that the active duty military income substituted for the income from the reservist's civilian job and the normal reserve pay from drills and annual training, and that all other sources of family income remained the same.[1] Military income includes basic pay, allowances for subsistence (BAS) and quarters (BAQ) and the tax advantages of these allowances, family separation pay, and variable housing allowances.[2]

The ODS survey was used to examine the pattern and distribution of income losses across mobilized reservists and to analyze their demand for income-protection insurance. The ODS data also provided unique information on additional expenses incurred by reservists during an actual mobilization. These data showed that reservists experienced large additional expenses, in addition to the more straightforward loss in income—something that could not have been estimated from the 1986 data.

ESTIMATED INCOME LOSSES FOR ALL RESERVISTS

Our estimates from the 1986 survey show that approximately 40 percent of all reserve officers and enlisted personnel would lose income during a hypothetical 12-month mobilization, assuming that military pay consists of basic pay and allowances, the tax advantage of al-

---

[1]The income loss estimates from the 1986 survey do not include estimates of continuing business losses after demobilization for self-employed individuals. Although a few may incur substantial losses when businesses incur continuing loss of good will, the overall estimates presented here will not be markedly affected by inclusion of such losses. If such losses are concentrated in certain pay grades, some bias may arise in estimates of losses by paygrade.

[2]The military income estimates do not include special pays such as combat zone pay or tax advantages granted to individuals in combat zones. Eligibility for combat pays are determined for each mobilization and depend on the definition of combat zones. Tax advantages must be granted by Congress and can occur after demobilization. Since reservists will be uncertain of receiving these advantages or pays and their amount, decisions about insurance purchase would probably not include these. The current estimates also do not include flight or medical pay. Pilots constitute less than 1 percent of all reservists, and physicians constitute only about one-half percent of reservists. So overall estimates of economic losses will not be significantly biased. However, since these individuals are more concentrated in the officer ranks of O-3 to O-6 and have substantially higher civilian incomes than typical reservists, a small downward bias in economic loss estimates will occur primarily among the group with higher economic losses. However, it should be noted that this bias may be offset partially by the omission of continuing business losses.

lowances, family separation pay, and variable housing allowances. Income loss is more frequent among higher paygrades, with almost 50 percent of O-4 to O-6 losing income and over 50 percent of E-6 to E-8 losing income. *For those losing income,* the median annual family income loss is approximately $11,000 for officers and $7,000 for enlisted personnel. *For those losing income,* the median percentage of family income loss is 17 percent for both officers and enlisted personnel. The median losses are particularly large for O-5 ($16,000) and O-6 ($32,000).

Some reservists suffer very large income losses. About 10 percent of all officers and enlisted personnel lose one-third or more of their family income. Two percent of all officers lose 50 percent or more of income and the same percentage of enlisted personnel lose 60 percent or more. The income losses for the highest 2 percent of losers are $46,000 or more for enlisted personnel and $57,000 or more for officers. The income losses are spread throughout all ranks and military occupations, although large losses are more frequent for higher-ranking personnel and those self-employed in the civilian sector.

RESERVE LOSSES DURING ODS

Survey data collected from ODS personnel indicate that income loss was more severe for those mobilized during ODS than that estimated from the 1986 survey. Approximately 55 percent of officers and 45 percent of enlisted personnel reported that they had income losses—these numbers are greater than the estimates of 40 percent cited above. This higher percentage may reflect the fact that those mobilized were higher in rank or came disproportionately from higher-income civilian occupations and tended to suffer more frequent and larger losses. It could also reflect the fact that the 1986 survey does not include business losses during mobilization or continuing losses after demobilization.

ODS data also showed that economic losses were not confined to lost income. Approximately 70 percent of enlisted personnel and 80 percent of officers indicated that they incurred additional expenses. These additional expenses were most frequently less than $2,500; however, 40 percent of officers and 25 percent of enlisted personnel incurred additional expenses of over $2,500. These additional expenses were often greater than income loss. Additional expenses could include costs associated with upkeep of medical practices or other types of offices, additional child care expenses, and other family expenses connected to the absence of the reservist. They could also include unreimbursed travel, quarters and subsistence costs, although military per diem payments usually cover these costs.

RESERVIST DEMAND FOR MOBILIZATION INSURANCE

A representative sample of reservists, including those participating in ODS, were asked about their interest in insurance protection against economic losses during mobilization. They were offered a choice of buying monthly income supplements ranging from $0 to $20,000 at two monthly premium levels: $0.40 per $100 and $1.00 per $100. Over 67 percent of enlisted personnel and 55 percent of officers said they would buy mobilization insurance if the monthly cost were $1.00 per $100 of coverage. Even more—73 percent of enlisted personnel and 60 percent of officers—said they would buy it at a lower price ($0.40 per $100 of coverage). Among those wanting to buy insurance, over 75 percent chose to buy from $500 to $2,000 of monthly benefits.

The degree of interest in insurance appears more than can be justified by lost income alone. Reservists probably were allowing for additional expenses as well as lost income. Interest was particularly high among junior personnel and this probably indicates that economic losses to them would have more dire consequences, perhaps because they lack savings or assets.

POLICY OPTIONS FOR PROVIDING MOBILIZATION INSURANCE

In developing options for insurance coverage, OSD should establish guidelines for coverage. These should include consideration of the following:

- All reservists should probably have the option of purchasing insurance.

- Insurance payments should probably begin immediately upon mobilization rather than through later reimbursement.

- Insurance premiums should be set at levels that result in purchases by reservists that would result in significant reduction in lost income during mobilization.

- Reservists should choose their amounts of coverage and pay at least part of the costs of such insurance.

- Restrictions on purchase are likely needed in periods of heightened tension when mobilization is likely.

Policymakers weighing various insurance programs to protect against such losses have three basic options: private insurance, government-provided insurance, or a joint private-sector/government arrangement. The insurance can also take two different forms. *Indemnity* insurance would require verification of losses for payments, and *value-form* would simply pay a specified amount without verification.

Several significant barriers exist for any single private insurer or groups of insurers to enter this market without government participation. First, actuarial data from which to estimate the risk of a callup, which is an important factor in establishing premiums and risk, are highly uncertain. Second, the risks being insured are highly correlated because there will be no losses in most years and large losses in others, a factor that often reduces the willingness of private companies to offer insurance coverage. Third, the amount of potential liability is very large and could be essentially unlimited for long mobilizations. Fourth, because some reservists may have better knowledge than private insurers of their risks of being mobilized, problems of adverse selection may arise. Adverse selection also occurs in time of crisis or mobilization and restrictions would be needed on the opportunity to buy insurance. Finally, because some reservists may be able to influence the probability that they will be mobilized through volunteering, moral hazard (that is, the fact that being insured may encourage risk-taking behavior) may be present in offering some forms of income-protection insurance.

Potential liability for a 6-month mobilization of 200,000 reservists would be between $1 billion and $1.5 billion, depending on desired purchase amounts in the survey. Furthermore, insurers would have to take account of the possibility of longer and larger mobilizations and would have to plan for more frequent mobilizations than indicated by historical data. Thus, private insurers would be facing very infrequent catastrophic losses but would be unable to accurately estimate either the size of a loss or its frequency.

Insurance that covers some type of wartime loss or other types of highly unpredictable catastrophic losses is usually structured with joint government/private participation (see Besen and Grissmer, 1992). Examples of such insurance are Servicemen's Group Life Insurance, which offers group life insurance for military personnel; nuclear accident insurance; flood insurance; and expropriation and riot insurance. In some cases, groups of private insurers provide limited insurance capacity with the government acting as a reinsurer for very large liabilities. In other cases, the government has assumed the entire risk and has used private insurers for administration only. However, business interruption insurance is provided solely by the private sector and covers lost income, including both lost profits and unavoidable expenses, and may offer some interesting lessons for the design of income-protection insurance that covers self-employed reservists against business losses during mobilization.

ISSUES FOR FURTHER STUDY

Our focus here has been on the adverse effects of mobilization on re-servists' financial well-being and one option for ameliorating these effects—income-protection insurance. However, several alternative policy solutions might solve the problem of income loss during mo-bilization. These include offering bonuses, or authorizing more comprehensive active duty fringe benefits. These will receive more attention in a future final report.

Several important issues still require study before income insurance could be offered. It will be important to design insurance in a way that does not discourage volunteering in times of crisis. If insurance covers volunteers, it will encourage volunteering. However, covering volunteers will increase the insurance risk from moral hazard and may raise premiums. Further study is required to determine whether volunteer decisions are influenced by considerations of economic gain or loss, and the extent of additional liability that insurers would have if volunteers are covered.

Other considerations include the tradeoffs among setting differential premiums based on different mobilization probabilities, determining when reservists can and cannot purchase insurance, and more generally determining specific forms and rules for such insurance that protect both reservists and insurers. Improved estimates of income losses that take into account special pays such as flight and medical pay will also be important, especially for pilots and physicians.

Further institutional study and consultation with the insurance and reserve communities will be required to develop specific plans or options for offering the insurance, should Congress and DoD decide to do so.

Chapter One

INTRODUCTION

Military reservists called to active duty may lose income because their active duty pay falls short of their civilian income or because of additional expenses incurred as a result of mobilization. Those most likely to lose large amounts of income are those in highly paid professions, such as physicians and pilots, or those who operate their own businesses. For such reservists, the Operation Desert Storm (ODS) experience showed that business losses may extend well beyond the end of mobilization because of the loss of client good will. However, losses may also occur across a broad spectrum of reservists in lower-income occupations. These losses may be smaller in magnitude, but their economic effect may be significant because these reservists may lack savings or may have fewer other options for mitigating the losses.

The threat of lost income during a mobilization could reduce the reserves' manpower supply—with potential larger declines in a few professional occupations—and adversely affect reserve readiness and performance. The magnitude of these potential effects depends partly on how many reservists sustain losses and how severe they are. The magnitude and type of economic losses will vary from one mobilization to another because different types of personnel will be called upon to serve. To be able to generalize across different types of mobilizations, it is necessary to characterize these economic losses for representative groups of reservists so that estimates of losses can be made across many different types of mobilizations, regardless of the mix of personnel involved.

It is also important to determine how widespread and large the losses are so policies can be tailored to fit the scope of the problem. If the income losses are confined to very few reservists in a few military occupations (physicians and pilots, for example), and economic loss patterns are fairly uniform, then compensation programs directed at mitigating the effects of economic loss on recruiting and retention can be targeted to these groups.   However, if the problem is widespread and falls across most military occupations, and if economic losses are highly variable, compensation programs would be less efficient because they could not be confined only to those suffering economic losses, and they would not have the flexibility to address the wide range of economic losses. In this case, insurance coverage has the potential to more effectively target those with economic losses and to have the flexibility to match the magnitude of individual losses.

Offering insurance protection has been suggested as a way to offset the adverse effects of economic losses on reservists and their families during mobilization (Grissmer et al., 1989). The feasibility of offering insurance will depend on how many reservists lose income and the amounts they lose, their interest in purchasing income-protection insurance, and the conditions required for private insurance carriers or the government to offer such insurance.

This report summarizes preliminary findings from an ongoing study examining reserve income loss following mobilization and the possibility of providing insurance against such losses. It provides preliminary estimates of the magnitude and distribution of reserve income losses for a hypothetical 12-month mobilization in which a representative sample of reservists is called up. It also provides estimates from the ODS mobilization, which lasted approximately 6 months and drew disproportionately from certain types of reserve personnel. The report also summarizes results from a study of the insurance industry and the current structure of several types of insurance that have similar risk structure to mobilization insurance.[1]

Specifically, the report addresses the following questions:

---

[1]For greater detail, see Besen and Grissmer (1992).

1. **Reserve Income Loss.** How many reservists would lose income if they were mobilized? How much income would they lose? What are the characteristics of the reservists who lose income? How did reserve losses during ODS compare to these estimates?

2. **Reservist Demand for Mobilization Insurance.** Would reservists buy insurance if it were offered? How many would purchase insurance? How much would they buy under different premiums?

3. **Providing and Structuring Mobilization Insurance.** What are the options for structuring income-protection insurance? How would insurance companies view such insurance? What are possible government roles? What criteria should government use in structuring such insurance?

Chapter Two estimates income losses that would occur for all reservists during callup and describes economic losses sustained by the group of reservists actually mobilized during ODS. Chapter Three projects the level of reservist demand for income-protection insurance. Chapter Four examines options for providing and structuring such insurance. Chapter Five offers preliminary conclusions and identifies unresolved questions surrounding these issues that will require further research.

Chapter Two

ECONOMIC LOSSES OF MOBILIZED RESERVISTS

This chapter contains two parts. The first characterizes income losses during a hypothetical 12-month mobilization for reservists who are representative of the entire Selected Reserve. It addresses three questions: (1) How many mobilized reservists would lose income? (2) How much does the typical reservist lose and what is the distribution of income losses across paygrades? (3) What are the characteristics of the reservists who lose income? The second part examines reported economic losses from those reservists mobilized during ODS. It presents estimates not only of lost income but of additional expenses as well.

We have intentionally separated our discussion of potential income losses for all reservists during mobilization from our discussion of reported losses during the ODS mobilization. Only selected portions of the total Reserve Force are called up during any particular mobilization and, therefore, neither ODS nor any other callup is likely to provide an accurate representation of the potential income-loss problem faced by all reservists. Income-protection insurance would probably be offered to all reservists and estimates of insurance demand and income losses must include all reservists—not merely those from a particular mobilization such as ODS.

In addition, the economic loss for an individual will vary across mobilizations and assignments in a mobilization because Congress and the Office of the Secretary of Defense (OSD) often establish policies, specific to a mobilization and specific to combat zones, that affect economic losses. These include establishing certain tax-free benefits to military pay received during a mobilization, declaring participants eligible for imminent danger pay, and increasing the extent and rapidity with which mobilized reservists are made eligible for certain active duty pay and allowances. Thus, data collected in ODS will reflect these specific policies; however, reservists purchasing insurance cannot count on receiving such benefits and would likely make decisions based on their absence.

The ODS survey does provides unique, experiential data on one aspect of economic loss previously ignored—losses stemming from additional expenses during mobilization. Income loss rather than additional expenses has been the focus of previous work attempting to estimate economic losses. ODS data show that additional expenses are an important part of the economic loss and are difficult to estimate without direct data gathered from actual experience.

INCOME LOSS ESTIMATES FROM THE *1986 SURVEY OF RESERVE FORCES*

We estimated reserve income losses using data from the *1986 Survey of Reserve Forces.*[1] The survey collected data on reservists' civilian income from all sources and the information required to estimate active duty pay. We supplemented the income data with tax rates for 1985, active and reserve base pay, reserve allowances, family separation pay, and Variable Housing Allowance (VHA) payments. The income and loss measures are expressed in terms of 1985 dollars.

Our measures of income loss are based on a 12-month callup for reservists. We first computed the annual civilian family income, which included the reservist's annual civilian pay, annual reserve pay, annual income from spouses, and other sources of family income. We have included annual reserve pay for drills and annual training as part of the civilian income estimate, since the reservists will lose this income upon mobilization. The 12-month family income during mobilization included active duty base pay, basic allowance for

---

[1]The survey population consisted of officers and enlisted personnel who were attending drills. This population excluded non-prior-service personnel at Initial Active Duty Training (IADT). The total survey sample selected for the survey consisted of 120,787 officers and enlisted personnel. A total of 63,687 completed surveys was obtained, which, after adjusting for ineligibles, provided a final response rate of 76 percent for officers and 60 percent for enlisted personnel.

subsistence (BAS) and quarters (BAQ) and the tax advantages of these allowances, family separation allowance, VHA, spousal income, and other family income sources. We assumed that the spouse would continue working and that other family income would continue unchanged.

Two potential sources of bias to our estimates of income losses may be partially offsetting, since they produce bias in opposite directions. We cannot estimate business losses or continuing income losses from loss of client good will that self-employed reservists or those in medical partnerships might experience. Such losses will occur for only a small proportion of reservists who usually have higher incomes. However, such losses might be substantial for this group. So this exclusion will bias estimates of median income loss downward for the self-employed or those who own businesses or participate as partners.

The current estimates also do not include special pays. Special pays can be divided into two classes: those that can be anticipated upon mobilization and those that cannot. The former includes pays such as hazardous duty pay, flight pay for pilots, or medical payments for health personnel. The latter includes combat zone pay and any tax advantages granted by Congress during or after mobilization.

In 1986, reservists who were mobilized could not draw hazardous duty, flight, or medical pay until they served longer than a year on active duty, so estimates for a 1986 mobilization would not include these pays. However, new legislation has significantly shortened the period of mobilization required to qualify for special pays.[2] There-

---

[2]Among special pays, hazardous duty pay affects a very small percentage of reservists and would not significantly affect economic loss estimates. Flight and medical pay are also drawn by very few reservists—approximately 1 percent. Although the ODS mobilization disproportionately mobilized physicians and pilots, the percentage of reservists mobilized who qualified for such pay still remained relatively small. For instance, of 250,000 reservists mobilized during ODS, less than 2 percent were physicians who would qualify for medical pay. Since these individuals are also among those who would have suffered the largest economic losses, flight and medical pay often would only reduce the amount lost—but not significantly change the percentage of reservists who lost income. However, since these individuals are concentrated in the officer ranks of O-3 to O-6, the estimates of median losses for these categories could be reduced somewhat by including special pays retroactively to 1986. However, this bias may be somewhat offset by leaving out business losses and continuing losses resulting from loss of good will.

fore, flight, medical, and hazardous duty pay should probably eventually be included in estimates, since these are more likely to be awarded. However, the exclusion of business losses and continuing business losses from loss of good will may partially or wholly offset the exclusion of medical and flight pay in the current estimates.

The reservists cannot count on certain types of special pays, such as combat zone and tax exempt status for pay, and would probably make insurance decisions based only on assured military pay. Therefore, income loss estimates used to evaluate insurance should also exclude these pays. We have also not included certain tax advantages granted to ODS personnel in combat zones. The pay of enlisted personnel and junior officers in combat zones was made tax free. Again, this exclusion cannot be counted on by reservists during peacetime, and insurance decisions would probably not be based on such exclusions.

RESULTS ON RESERVE INCOME LOSSES

How Many Reservists Lose Income During Mobilization?

As Figure 1 shows, approximately 40 percent of all reservists lose income during a 12-month mobilization. The totals are roughly equivalent for officers (39.1 percent) and enlisted personnel (38.8 percent). A greater proportion of officers at higher pay grades have income losses. At the three highest paygrades, approximately 45 percent lose income, compared with only 25.9 percent at the lowest paygrade.

More enlisted reservists in the mid-range paygrades (E-5 to E-7) have income losses than more junior or more senior personnel: 54.2 percent in the E-7 grade lose income, compared with 23.3 percent at E-3 and 45.7 percent at E-9.

How Much Income Do They Lose?

This part of the analysis focuses on the group of reservists losing income, since this group will determine the demand for mobilization insurance. Income losses need to be measured both in absolute and in relative terms. A given loss in income may not be as serious for those with high incomes as for those with low incomes. Here, we measure loss in terms of annual income loss and percentage of

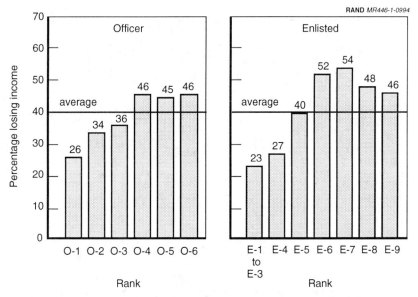

Figure 1—Percentage of Reservists Losing Income upon Mobilization

family income lost. We present the median distribution of income loss *only for that group of reservists losing income.* As noted above, this group includes approximately 40 percent of officers and enlisted personnel. Absolute income losses tend to be larger for the more senior paygrades among both officers and enlisted personnel. However, percentage income losses for enlisted personnel tend to be higher for those at lower ranks.

Officers. Figure 2 characterizes income losses for officers who lose income in both dollar and percentage terms. For officers losing income, the median loss across all paygrades is $10,800, or 17.7 percent of family income. The O-6 grade loses the highest amount in both dollar terms ($31,800) and percentage terms (26.9 percent). Although the actual dollar amount lost by officers in the lowest paygrade is much smaller, approximately $8,000, in percentage terms the losses are quite substantial: 21.5 percent of income.

Figures 3 and 4 show the cumulative distribution of income losses both in dollar and percentage terms for reserve officers losing

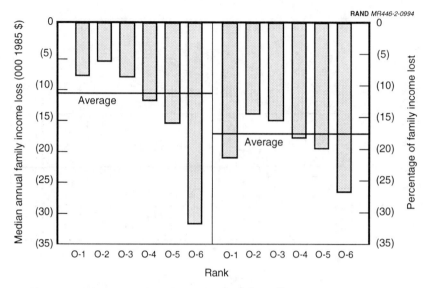

**Figure 2—Characterizing Income Losses for Officers Losing Income:
12-Month Mobilization**

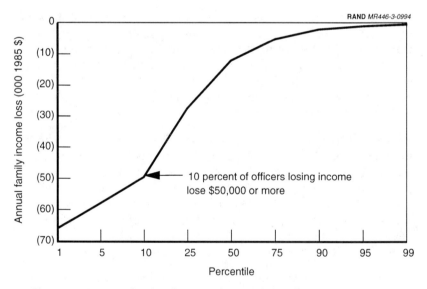

**Figure 3—Percentile Distribution of Annual Family Income Lost for
Officers Losing Income: 12-Month Mobilization**

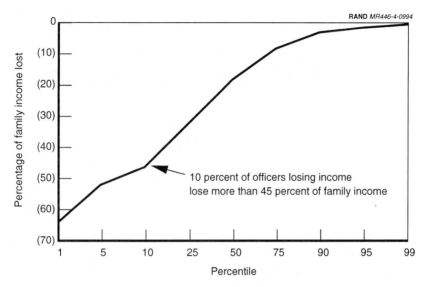

Figure 4—Distribution of Percentage of Family Income Lost for Officers
Losing Income: 12-Month Mobilization

income. The distribution is presented in percentile terms. As Figure
3 shows, approximately half of the reserve officers who lose
incomesustain losses of approximately $10,800 or less; 25 percent
lose more than $27,000; and 5 percent lose more than $57,000. In
percentage terms, as shown in Figure 4, 50 percent of income-losing
reserve officers lose 18 percent or less of income; 25 percent lose
more than 31 percent; and 5 percent lose more than 52 percent.

Enlisted Personnel. Figure 5 shows income losses for enlisted reserve personnel *who lose income* expressed in both dollar and percentage terms. For enlisted personnel, the median dollar loss across
all paygrades is $6,300. The figure is highest for E-9 ($8,600) and
smallest for E-1 and E-2 personnel ($5,200). In percentage terms,
however, the lowest paygrades sustain the largest losses: 20.5 percent for E-3, 18.5 percent for E-4, 18.6 percent for E-5, compared with
only 14.6 percent for E-9. Figures 6 and 7 show the percentile distribution of income losses for enlisted reservists in dollar and percentage terms, respectively. As Figure 6 shows, half of enlisted personnel
who lose income incur losses of less than $8,000, 25 percent lose
more than $12,000, and 5 percent lose more than $46,000. In

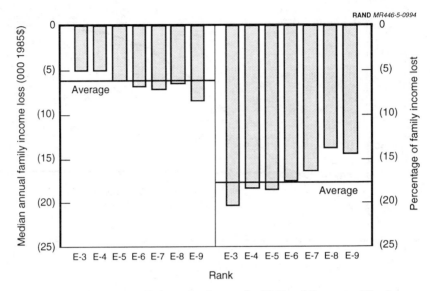

Figure 5—Characterizing Income Losses for Enlisted Personnel Losing
Income: 12-Month Mobilization

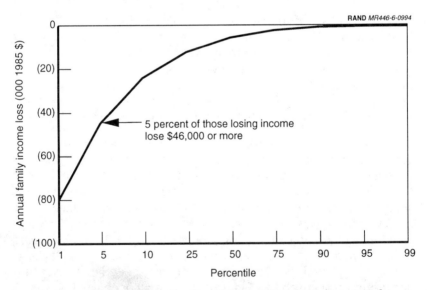

Figure 6—Percentile Distribution of Annual Family Income Lost for
Enlisted Personnel Losing Income: 12-Month Mobilization

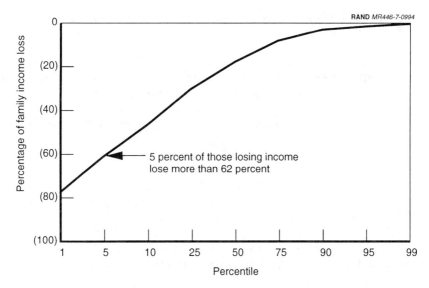

Figure 7—Distribution of Percentage of Family Income Lost for Enlisted
Personnel Losing Income: 12-Month Mobilization

percentage terms, as Figure 7 shows, 50 percent of enlisted reservists
who incur losses lose less than 20 percent of income, 25 percent of
enlisted reservists lose more than 31 percent of income, and 5
percent of enlisted reservists lose more than 62 percent of income.

Summary. If we view the income losses as a percentage of all officers
(both those losing and those not losing income), the data from Figures 1–4 show that income losses greater than 10 percent of family
income would occur for approximately 30 percent of all officers and
income losses greater than 30 percent of family income would occur
for about 10 percent of officers. In addition, about 2 percent of officers have income losses greater than 50 percent of family income.

Similarly, including all enlisted personnel (those losing and those not
losing income), the combined results of Figure 1 and Figures 5–7
show that approximately 30 percent of all enlisted personnel lose 10
percent or more of family income and 10 percent lose more than 30
percent of family income. In addition, approximately 5 percent of all
enlisted reservists lose more than 50 percent of family income.

What Are the Characteristics of the Reservists Who Lose Income?

Table 1 shows the characteristics of reserve officers who experience either large income losses, small income losses, or none. We characterized "large losses" as amounts above 10 percent of family income. The group experiencing no loss will include personnel not in the labor force, such as students or homemakers, those currently unemployed, as well as those having jobs that result in net income gains during mobilization.

Not surprisingly, officers with larger percentage income losses tend to have higher civilian family incomes. Their mean family income is $78,100; these figures are substantially higher than the mean income for the entire group of $54,100. For officers, self-employment is the characteristic with the highest risk for large income loss. The self-employed constitute 18.9 percent of large income losers compared to

Table 1

Which Officers Lose Income? Differences in Characteristics

Characteristic	Non-Losers	Small Income Loss	Large Income Loss	All
Mean family income, $	42,000	60,000	78,100	54,100
Percentage married	73.2	83.4	79.0	76.0
Percentage male	84.4	92.4	94.5	88.1
Average rank	3.24	3.44	3.61	3.37
Average years of service	13.3	14.0	14.2	13.6
Percentage federal employees	12.9	15.6	11.0	12.7
Percentage state employees	11.8	8.9	6.3	10.0
Percentage local government employees	10.3	9.2	5.3	8.8
Percentage self-employed	10.2	9.1	18.9	12.5
Percentage large firm	26.3	42.2	42.1	32.5
Percentage medium firm	7.9	7.1	7.1	7.6
Percentage small firm	12.4	7.3	8.5	10.7
Percentage spouse working full-time	42.0	42.2	27.1	37.9
Percentage tactical operation	31.0	32.8	33.3	31.8
Percentage intelligence	4.9	6.3	2.8	4.5
Percentage engineering and maintenance	12.9	13.3	11.3	12.6
Percentage scientists and professionals	6.2	6.6	7.0	6.4
Percentage health care	16.3	14.4	20.9	17.4
Percentage administrators	15.7	15.1	14.0	15.2
Percentage supply and procurement	8.9	7.9	7.1	8.2

only 12.5 percent of all reservists. Those working in a military health-care occupation or working at a large firm are at somewhat greater risk of sustaining large income losses. Conversely, officers with spouses working full-time, those working for state or local government, and those working in small firms are less likely to sustain large percentage losses. Spousal income tends to be a cushioning factor against larger income losses. Spouses with children may reduce work hours in the absence of the reservists, although we assume that spousal income will continue during mobilization.

Table 2 shows the characteristics of enlisted reservists who experience large, small, or no income losses. Again, these are defined in terms of percentage income lost (more than 10 percent, 1–10 percent, 0 percent). The mean family income of enlisted personnel who incur large percentage losses is $44,900, as compared with $28,100

Table 2

Which Enlisted Personnel Lose Income? Differences in Characteristics

Characteristic	Non-Losers	Small Losers	Large Losers	All
Mean family income, $	19,100	35,300	44,900	28,100
Percentage married	55.3	75.9	70.0	61.6
Percentage male	87.2	93.9	94.7	90.0
Average pay grade	4.8	5.4	5.3	5.0
Mean years of service	8.9	11.7	11.5	9.9
Percentage federal employees	7.0	15.2	15.8	10.3
Percentage state employees	7.8	9.9	7.0	7.8
Percentage local government employees	6.5	10.7	10.0	8.0
Percentage self-employed	9.8	5.5	6.5	8.4
Percentage large firm	18.8	28.9	36.0	24.7
Percentage medium firm	12.6	12.4	9.9	11.9
Percentage small firm	23.5	15.0	12.2	19.4
Percentage spouse working full-time	28.0	40.1	28.7	29.7
Percentage combat	23.7	19.6	17.5	21.5
Percentage electronic repair	3.0	4.4	5.5	3.8
Percentage communications and intelligence	8.4	8.2	8.2	8.3
Percentage health care	6.2	5.5	4.6	5.7
Percentage technical specialist	3.7	4.6	4.2	4.0
Percentage support and administration	18.9	21.3	20.6	19.6
Percentage electric/mechanical repair	15.4	16.4	18.5	16.3
Percentage craftsman	6.4	7.1	7.6	6.8
Percentage service and supply	12.9	11.6	12.1	12.6

for all enlisted reserves. Federal employees and those working in large firms are at greatest risk for higher percentage losses; however, self-employed enlisted personnel—unlike officers—have less chance of large losses. The nature of the military occupation for enlisted personnel does not appear to have a substantial effect on whether large percentage income losses occur. The enlisted group not losing income includes a larger proportion than the officer group of those not in the labor force, such as students and homemakers and also those who are unemployed or employed part-time.

RESERVE INCOME LOSSES DURING OPERATION DESERT STORM

How does this picture of potential reserve losses compare to the experience of reservists mobilized during ODS? To answer this question, we analyzed data from a survey of reservists called to active duty during ODS.[3] The survey had questions on both income loss and additional unreimbursed expenses occurring during ODS. It also contained questions concerning interest in income-protection insurance and the desired amount of insurance under two different premiums.

---

[3]The survey was conducted during late 1991–early 1992. The survey population consisted of all reserve personnel who were in the Selected Reserve as of March 1991, stratified by reserve component, by officer/enlisted rank, by mobilized/nonmobilized status, and by military/nonmilitary health-care profession. Mobilized reservists, especially health-care professionals, were oversampled, as there was a great deal of concern regarding their income losses and general experience during ODS. The stratified random survey sample consisted of approximately 20,000 military reservists and 20,000 nonmilitary reservists, equally divided between mobilized and nonmobilized groups, who received different questionnaires (Form 1 and Form 2). Overall response rates (percentage of those responding among the eligible sample) were about 70 percent. However, sampling errors discovered after the fielding of the survey in the identification and categorization of the survey population and the necessary steps taken to correct these errors have delayed the publication of official weights that would allow us to generalize from the survey respondents to all reservists. Instead, we have, for purposes of this analysis, made a simple correction for nonresponse by using a technique called poststratification weighting. This technique basically uses information on the distribution of the survey population over different subgroups (in this case the stratification variables) and the response rates to create a weight such that the distribution of the weighted respondent sample conforms to that of the original survey population. See Kalton (1983) for further details, and Grissmer et al. (1984) for an application of this method.

The results show that a higher percentage of ODS reservists reported some income loss than we estimated would be the case in a hypothetical callup, based on the 1986 survey. Figure 8 compares the percentage reporting income losses from the two survey samples. Using the 1986 data, we project that approximately 39 percent of officers and enlisted personnel would lose income during a hypothetical 12-month mobilization. During ODS, approximately 55 percent of officers and 45 percent of enlisted personnel indicated some income loss. However, the pattern of losses across different ranks for the ODS data was similar to that in the 1986 survey data. Higher-ranking officers and midlevel enlisted personnel were more likely to lose income in both surveys.

The ODS estimates might differ from the 1986 loss estimates for several reasons. First, the percentage losing income in ODS might be expected to be higher than shown in the 1986 survey because the mobilization called up a disproportionately high share of personnel having higher civilian incomes. Reservists mobilized tended to be combat support or service support personnel with higher pay grades than combat personnel. The mobilization also disproportionately

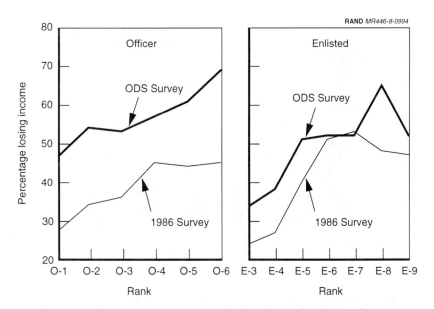

Figure 8—Reserve Income Losses During Operation Desert Storm

called up pilots and medical personnel who would have higher civilian incomes.

The ODS data differ from the estimates provided by the 1986 survey in three other ways. The ODS estimates presumably included consideration of any company policies to continue normal or lower levels of pay while the employee was mobilized. The estimates from the 1986 survey assumed no civilian pay during mobilization. However, preliminary analysis shows that only a very small percentage of employers provided continuing pay to reservists during ODS. Second, these estimates would also presumably account for some continuing business losses. Finally, special pays such as hazardous duty, flight, medical and combat zone, and tax advantages granted by Congress, may also be included in the ODS estimates.

Figures 9 and 10 show the distribution of ODS income losses as well as estimates of additional expenses. Turning to income losses first, we find that between 45–55 percent of reservists did not have any income losses. However, some suffered substantial amounts of lost income. For example, among officers, about 24 percent had income losses of $5,000–$25,000 and 15 percent had income losses of over

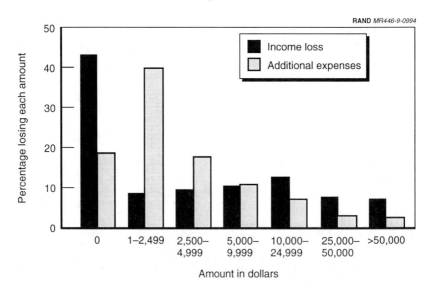

Figure 9—Lost Income and Additional Expenses of Officers in Operation Desert Storm

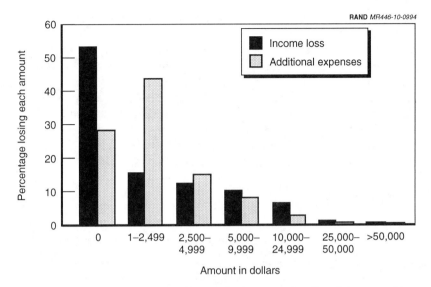

Figure 10—Lost Income and Additional Expenses of Enlisted Personnel in
Operation Desert Storm

$25,000. Among the enlisted, about 17 percent had income losses of
$5,000–$25,000 and a small percentage, less than 2 percent, had
income losses of over $25,000. These losses cannot be compared to
the 1986 estimates because they assume different periods of
mobilization. The ODS losses were sustained over amuch shorter
period of mobilization than the one-year period assumed in the 1986
survey calculations. Further analysis is required to convert the two
income loss estimates to a common time basis. Not only must the
difference in the length of mobilization be taken into account, but
also the differences in the characteristics of ODS personnel and
average reservists and the differences in family income sources
between 1986 and 1990–1991. Also, adjustments to the same real
level of dollars must be made.

Perhaps the most important result from ODS is the importance of
additional expenses in estimating total economic loss. Figures 9 and
10 show that reservists indicated that additional expenses were a
significant source of economic loss. Some additional expenses occurred for 80 percent of officers and 70 percent of enlisted personnel.
Most losses were between $1 and $2,500, but 40 percent of officers

and 25 percent of enlisted personnel indicated additional expenses of $2,500 or more. For many of the reservists, these expenses exceeded the amount of income lost, especially at the smallest levels of income loss. The survey did not identify the sources of the additional expenses. They could have arisen from expenses associated with the upkeep of medical practices or other types of businesses, or from additional expenses of child care, health care, or other family living expenses. Some reservists may not have been fully reimbursed for living expenses when assigned away from their duty stations, although per diem rates were paid to reservists and these generally provide sufficient compensation to offset food and lodging costs.[4]

---

[4]Some interesting insights are gained from the results of a survey of Naval Reserve physicians and dentists conducted by Ken Coffey of the U.S. Naval Academy. He surveyed 693 physicians and 74 dentists who were recalled to active duty. Overall, 59 percent said they were required to pay ongoing office and professional expenses; this was true of almost all of the orthopedic surgeons and dental general practitioners. Estimated amounts for these latter groups were well over $100,000. About 77 percent of the respondents said they had lost income while mobilized and for those in private practices, estimates of loss ranged from $75,000 to $200,000. Given these large amounts, surprisingly, more than two-thirds of those surveyed said they were not considering leaving the Naval Reserve; there were no significant differences in the average loss of those who were considering resigning versus those who intended to stay (see Coffey, 1992).

Chapter Three

DEMAND FOR MOBILIZATION INSURANCE

This chapter estimates reservist demand for income-protection insurance using survey data collected from mobilized and nonmobilized reservists after ODS. The data are weighted to be representative of the entire Reserve Force.[1]

HOW MANY WOULD BUY INSURANCE?

We presented reservists with options of buying income-protection insurance with monthly payments beginning when mobilized (as indicated in Table 3). We asked them how much they would purchase under premium levels of $0.40 per $100 of monthly income supplement and $1.00 per $100 of income supplement.[2]

Figure 11 shows the percentage of officers and enlisted personnel, categorized by paygrade, who indicate that they would purchase some insurance. The results show broad interest in purchasing income protection. Approximately 55 percent of officers and 65 percent of enlisted personnel indicate interest in purchasing some

---

[1]See footnote 3 in Chapter Two for details on how the weights were estimated.

[2]The premium amounts were approximated using a simple actuarial model that estimated the insurance premiums required to fairly fund the long-term costs of callups, assuming their historical frequency, duration, and magnitude. Since the ODS data were not available to make estimates of losses, we used the 1986 survey and assumed that all reservists losing income would purchase insurance exactly equal to their income loss. Additional work is ongoing to develop a more complex and accurate model based on more recent data from ODS.

Table 3

Insurance Questions on Survey

Q59. Some have suggested that insurance companies could provide mobilization insurance to pay reservists additional monthly income during a mobilization. Such income would be in addition to your active duty income. If available, would you be interested in buying such insurance to cover losses in income or pay additional expenses when mobilized?

1. Yes
2. Not sure
3. No (GO TO QUESTION 62)

Q60. If you could buy such insurance through monthly withholding from your reserve paycheck, how much additional monthly income during mobilization would you buy if the monthly costs were as given below?

1. None
2. $100 a month for 40 cents of monthly pay
3. $250 a month for $1 of monthly pay
4. $500 a month for $2 of monthly pay
5. $1,000 a month for $4 of monthly pay
6. $2,000 a month for $8 of monthly pay
7. $5,000 a month for $20 of monthly pay
8. $10,000 a month for $40 of monthly pay
9. $20,000 a month for $80 of monthly pay

Q61. Suppose the rates were higher as indicated below. How much insurance would you buy?

1. None
2. $100 a month for $1 of monthly pay
3. $250 a month for $2.50 of monthly pay
4. $500 a month for $5 of monthly pay
5. $1,000 a month for $10 of monthly pay
6. $2,000 a month for $20 of monthly pay
7. $5,000 a month for $50 of monthly pay
8. $10,000 a month for $100 of monthly pay
9. $20,000 a month for $100 of monthly pay

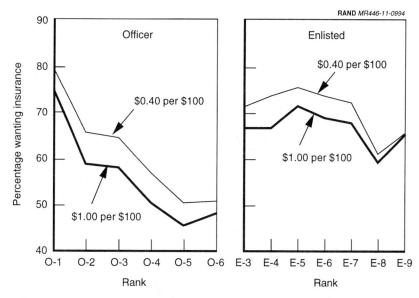

Figure 11—Percentage Wanting to Buy Insurance at Two Premium Levels

amount of insurance at the lower premium level. The demand falls by about 5 percentage points at the higher premium level.

The data suggest that junior officers have significantly greater interest than senior officers, whereas interest among enlisted personnel is approximately the same for E-3 through E-7. These results show a higher interest than would be indicated by income losses alone. This might be explained if insurance is being bought to cover additional expenses as well as income loss. It may also reflect the fact that reservists would base decisions to buy insurance not simply on current income, but on the possibility that job changes and advancement would place them at greater risk in future mobilizations. Thus, they may buy more insurance than current job and wages would justify. Another factor could be the possibility of compensating for nonpecuniary losses associated with mobilization. This would include the stress of family separation and risks of injury or fatality. Finally, the stronger interest among junior personnel might reflect lower levels of savings and other resources available to cushion losses.

HOW MUCH WOULD THEY BUY?

We asked the ODS reservists how much insurance they would buy at each of the two premium levels. The results are shown in Figures 12 and 13.

Officers

About 40 percent of officers do not want to purchase any insurance at the price of $0.40 per $100. This percentage rises to about 45 percent when the price rises to $1.00 per $100. Of those wanting to purchase at the two prices, about 75 percent wish to purchase income supplements ranging from $500 to $2,000. The median amount bought is $1,000 of monthly income supplement. About 5 percent of officers wished to purchase $10,000 or more of monthly coverage.

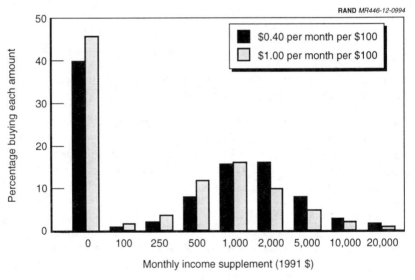

Figure 12—Amount of Insurance Desired by Officers: Two Premium Levels

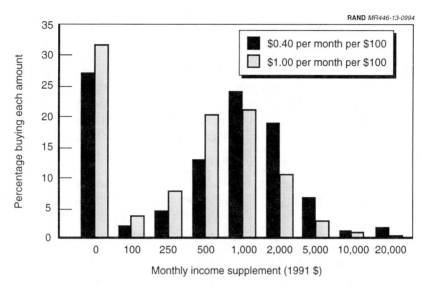

Figure 13—Amount of Insurance Desired by Enlisted Personnel: Two
Premium Levels

Enlisted Personnel

A much larger proportion of enlisted personnel indicated interest in buying some insurance. Only about 27 percent of enlisted personnel (compared to 40 percent of officers) said they would not purchase any at the lower price; this proportion rises slightly to 32 percent at the higher price. The median amount desired by enlisted personnel was $1,000, as it was with officers; the majority would purchase insurance that would provide income supplements of between $500 and $2,000. About 3 percent of enlisted personnel would purchase $10,000 or more of monthly coverage.

SUMMARY

The 1986 survey data revealed that about 40 percent of reservists would lose income if mobilized. The ODS survey data showed that about 55 percent of officers and 45 percent of enlisted personnel reported income losses—probably indicating that income losers were more likely to be called in this mobilization. However, ODS survey data also showed that economic losses were not confined to income losses; significant levels of additional expenses were reported.   If these reports are accurate, then approximately two-thirds of reservists called up suffered economic losses.

Thus, the strong interest in insurance protection is not surprising. Over 60 percent of officers and 70 percent of enlisted personnel indicated a desire to purchase some insurance at the lower premium of $0.40 per $100 of monthly coverage.   This level drops only about 5 percentage points with a higher premium of $1.00 per $100 of monthly coverage.   Interest in purchasing insurance is stronger among junior officers and all enlisted personnel. Among those desiring to purchase insurance, most choose monthly coverage levels of between $500 and $2,000. Given this widespread demand for insurance coverage, the design of a program becomes important.   The next chapter provides preliminary analysis of design options.

Chapter Four

OPTIONS FOR OFFERING INSURANCE

This chapter suggests several guidelines for structuring income-pro-. tection insurance and examines various options for providing reserve income-protection insurance.[1] It first discusses possible guidelines and the two types of insurance that could be offered: *indemnity* coverage and *value-form* coverage. It then explores three options for providing such insurance: solely through the private sector, solely through government intervention, or jointly.

DESIGN CRITERIA FOR INCOME-PROTECTION INSURANCE

From a public policy perspective, insurance programs for covering income losses during mobilization have several desirable features.

All reservists should have the option of purchasing insurance. The previous analysis has shown that the economic losses encountered by reservists are not confined to a few military occupations or those with high levels of civilian income. Insurance plans that offer coverage selectively to any group of reservists will not address the widespread nature of the problem, nor will it be equitable to give some reservists the option to purchase insurance and not others. The option to buy insurance coverage should then be available to all reservists.

Insurance payments should begin immediately upon mobilization rather than through later reimbursement. The financial stress for

---

[1]This chapter draws from the detailed discussion in Besen and Grissmer (1992).

many reservists and their families can begin shortly after mobilization. The program should begin income payments as soon after mobilization as possible rather than through reimbursement.

Insurance premiums should be set at levels that result in purchases by reservists that would significantly reduce lost income during mobilization. Insurance programs with premiums that result in inadequate coverage of most reserve income loss would not be effective in offsetting the potential adverse effects of mobilization on recruiting and retention. Moreover, such programs would have coverage based on ability to pay in peacetime and would probably result in differential coverage by income level.

Reservists should choose their amounts of coverage and pay at least part of the costs of such insurance. Since the reservist alone knows the amount of insurance required to cover any income loss, the reservist should make the choice of amount of insurance coverage. Cost-sharing by reservists would discourage overcoverage and would result in a more efficient choice of coverage amounts.

Restrictions on purchase are needed in periods of heightened tension when mobilization is likely. Allowing open purchase of insurance during periods of heightened tensions creates adverse selection and substantially increases the costs of insurance to all. Insurance purchases need to be restricted to clearly defined occasions such as enlistment or reenlistment after an initial open enrollment period. New enlistees may be given the option of coverage regardless of the level of tensions.

TYPES OF COVERAGE

Broadly speaking, two types of insurance could be offered to reservists. The first type would seek to replace all or a portion of actual dollar losses experienced by a mobilized reservist. This type of coverage is known in the insurance industry as *indemnity* coverage. This type of coverage poses difficulties for reservists in that they would be required to document their actual losses. It also creates some administrative costs for insurers in verifying these losses.

The second type of insurance would pay benefits based not on actual losses but on the amount of coverage to which the reservist had subscribed. This type of coverage is referred to in the industry as *value-form* coverage. Reservists would simply receive monthly income supplements upon mobilization with no verification of loss required. Reservists might be permitted to subscribe to any amount of coverage, or limits might be placed on the coverage provided. The same limits could apply to all reservists or could vary for different reservists, depending perhaps on their military occupations. Hybrid plans could also be structured that would require verification only for large losses.

Given the diverse nature of economic losses that reservists face, the value-form coverage is probably preferable. Some economic loss results from simple income differences that might be verified. However, losses from self-owned business, forgone commissions or bonuses, or additional expenses might be hard and laborious to verify. Since these types of losses make up an important part of reserve losses, payments independent of verification would be preferred. Requiring no verification would also allow payments to start immediately upon mobilization when the money would be needed. However, significant cost-sharing by reservists would also be required in value-form coverage to prevent reservists from subscribing to amounts of insurance significantly greater than the economic losses they faced.

THE PRIVATE SECTOR AS SOLE PROVIDER

Providing income-protection insurance would not be a simple decision for private-sector insurers, and obtaining the insurance capacity to cover all reservists wishing to purchase insurance is not straightforward for several reasons. First, actuarial data from which to estimate the risk of a callup—an important factor in establishing premiums and risk—are not available. Second, the risks being insured are highly correlated because there will be no losses in most years and large losses in others, a factor that often reduces the willingness of private companies to offer insurance coverage. Third, the amount of potential liability is very large and could be essentially unlimited for long mobilizations. Fourth, because some reservists may have better knowledge than private insurers of their risks of being mobilized, problems of adverse selection may arise. Adverse selection also occurs in time of crisis or mobilization and restrictions would be needed on the opportunity to buy insurance. Finally, because some reservists may be able to influence the probability that they will be mobilized through volunteering, moral hazard (that is, the fact that being insured may encourage risk-taking behavior) may be present in offering some forms of income-protection insurance.

Volunteering was an important initial source of mobilization manpower in ODS. As such, insurance should be designed that does not discourage volunteers. This might mean that coverage would occur for either volunteering or mobilization.   However, overall premiums would have to rise to cover the risk from moral hazard.

Potential liability for a mobilization of 6 months of 200,000 reservists would be between $1 billion and $1.5 billion, depending on desired purchase amounts in the survey. Furthermore, insurers would have to take account of the possibility of longer and larger mobilizations and would have to plan for more frequent mobilizations than indicated by historical data. Thus, private insurers could face very infrequent catastrophic losses, but would be unable to accurately estimate either the size of a loss or its frequency.

We have studied current insurance markets to find insurance situations with a similar risk structure to see how private-sector insurers respond to such situations. We find that income-protection insurance for military reservists would be a unique situation in insurance markets, although other forms of insurance that have some common elements of risk structure can serve as a guide for structuring such insurance.

LESSONS FROM ANALOGOUS TYPES OF INSURANCE

The types of insurance involving highly uncertain but potentially large risks include nuclear accident insurance, life insurance coverage for war deaths, marine and shipping insurance in times of hostility, business and property insurance in high crime and riot areas, flood insurance, earthquake insurance, expropriation insurance, business interpretation insurance, and crop insurance. We have studied how each of these types of insurance is structured—particularly in terms of the private-sector and government roles. We briefly describe some of these types of insurance and then summarize lessons learned for structuring income-protection insurance.

Servicemen's Group Life Insurance

An instructive parallel can be found in the group life insurance plan for military personnel (Servicemen's Group Life Insurance, or SGLI). SGLI is provided through a joint effort of the federal government and private insurance carriers. In this arrangement, private carriers bear a limited amount of risk for normal levels of peacetime deaths, but the federal government bears the risk for deaths that exceed preset levels of peacetime death. This means that the federal government bears the risks for wartime death rates and any extraordinary peacetime death rates. Since the inception of SGLI, the government has made payments to cover deaths only during the Vietnam War.

The limited peacetime risk is shared among many insurance carriers through reinsurance, and Prudential serves as the chief administrative agent for the plan. Premium rates are established jointly by government and private-sector actuaries and are set to provide sufficient reserves to maintain death payments for reasonable variations in death rates. Private-sector insurers receive negotiated "fees" for their participation in the plan.

Participation in SGLI while voluntary is nearly universal among active duty personnel. This universal coverage is achieved through a "negative checkoff" procedure that assumes coverage will be accepted and payroll deductions made unless the service member takes specific action to stop the process.

It is important to realize that in this plan private insurers do not bear risks associated with the occurrence of war. This is also the case for maritime insurance during periods of hostilities. The government has been the traditional reinsurer of wartime death and maritime risks because private-sector insurers presumably were unwilling to assume such risks.

Nuclear Accident Insurance

In the case of nuclear accident insurance, private-sector insurers were also unwilling to provide coverage without government participation. The Price-Anderson Act established three layers of responsibilities for nuclear accidents. A first layer was provided by private insurers, but private insurer liability was capped. A second layer was provided collectively by utilities owning nuclear power plants. Liability above these levels was provided by the government. The government provided the necessary legislation and "umbrella" under which private insurers were willing to enter the market and assume a limited part of the liability for nuclear accidents.

Flood, Riot, and Crime Insurance

The government role in providing certain types of flood insurance is very different. The government bears the entire risk for certain types of flood insurance, and private-sector carriers serve as administrative agents for marketing and paying policies. In the case of riot insurance, insurance pools are organized by private carriers in each state to provide property insurance to applicants who cannot obtain insurance in the private market. However, the government reinsures approximately 90 percent of losses sustained by carriers. Crime insurance is also provided to businesses that cannot buy burglary and robbery insurance in the private sector and the federal government bears the entire risk for this program.

U.S.-Owned Property Overseas

In the case of insurance against damage or loss of U.S. business property in foreign countries, the government established the Overseas Private Investors Corporation (OPIC). This agency provides protection against expropriation, war, insurrection, and confiscation. Coverage is limited in amount and to countries having agreements with the United States.

Business Interruption Insurance

Business interruption insurance provided solely by the private sector covers lost income—including both lost profits and unavoidable expenses—resulting from periods when businesses cannot operate because of accidents. This type of insurance affords two interesting lessons for reservists' income-protection insurance. First, insurers are willing, at least in some cases, to cover losses that arise when a business is unable to operate. Losses accrued by self-employed reservists are an important part of the problem we are analyzing, and these losses are more difficult to estimate and document than salary losses. However, the availability of business interruption insurance indicates that these kinds of losses can probably be covered in any mobilization insurance plan. Second, business interruption insurers are willing, at least in some circumstances, to pay benefits that are based not on the actual loss sustained but on the amount of insurance to which the policyholder has subscribed. The existence of these types of policies indicates that such arrangements are feasible. Moreover, this form of coverage avoids the need for any costly determinations of actual losses.

These analogous situations indicate that private insurers would probably require some conditions and sharing of risks before agreeing to offer income-protection coverage. At least four conditions will probably be required. First, the risk of loss would have to be spread over a large number of carriers through reinsurance, so that no single carrier bears a large portion of the risk. The insurance capacity to cover all reservists willing to buy insurance is substantial, and a large consortium of companies similar to SGLI would probably be required. Second, government reinsurance will probably be required to protect against very large losses incurred through unusually frequent, large, or long mobilizations. This will establish the maximum liability that a carrier can incur during a given period of time. Third, some protection of carriers from problems of adverse selection and moral hazard would probably be required. Finally, private carriers may offer the insurance only if they can combine it in a portfolio of other risks that are difficult to assess.

POSSIBLE GOVERNMENT ROLES

The government could provide mobilization insurance itself or help private firms provide such coverage. A reasonable inference is that premiums would have to be substantially higher without government reinsurance if coverage was provided at all. If this inference is correct, it suggests that some form of government support, perhaps in the form of reinsurance, may be necessary to obtain private-sector participation in providing income-protection insurance to military reservists with premiums at affordable levels for reservists.

Government as Sole Provider

If private insurers prove unwilling to offer income-protection insurance, the federal government would have to offer it. Furthermore, even if private firms are willing, the government may wish to offer the coverage itself. For example, the government may face lower administrative costs, probably possesses superior estimates of potential losses and differential probabilities of mobilization, and can likely accept a smaller risk premium.

Government as Partner

The government could also subsidize private insurance or act as reinsurer. The government may wish to play such a role for several reasons. First, government reinsurance may permit limits to be placed on the risks borne by private insurers, which would make offering such coverage more attractive to private carriers. Second, government subsidies of insurance premiums may also encourage private firms to offer coverage and reservists to purchase it. Third, the government may wish to require the purchase of some insurance by all reservists to avoid having large numbers of reservists experience losses in future mobilizations. Fourth, the government may be able to help private carriers reduce administrative costs by contracting for a group policy for all reservists.

Chapter Five

PRELIMINARY CONCLUSIONS AND ISSUES FOR FURTHER RESEARCH

This chapter highlights our preliminary findings, discusses their implications, and identifies issues for further research.

RESERVE INCOME LOSSES

We estimate that a sizable fraction of reservists—approximately 40 percent of both officers and enlisted personnel—stand to lose income during a 12-month mobilization. In our estimates, we assumed that reservists received military pay and allowances, family separation pay, and variable housing allowances. These estimates of loss, however, do not include special pays such as combat zone pay, hazardous duty pay, flight pay, or medical pay. On the other hand, we do not take into account continuing business losses after mobilization. These exclusions will be partially offsetting but will affect only a small minority of reserve personnel who have higher than average civilian incomes. Including these factors would only slightly reduce the percentage of reservists losing income, but may bias the median income lost, especially for senior officers.

About one-fourth of those losing income—that is, about 10 percent of the total Reserve Force—could potentially sustain large losses, upward of 30 percent of their civilian income. These potential losses are concentrated among officers and enlisted personnel in the highest paygrades. They also disproportionately affect civilians who are self-employed, but lower-ranking officers and enlisted personnel can also lose a significant percentage of their family income, although their absolute dollar losses are smaller than those of senior officers.

35

During ODS, an even higher percentage of mobilized reservists lost income, perhaps because those most prone to income loss are more likely to be mobilized. Approximately 45 percent of enlisted personnel and 55 percent of officers reported income losses. Many ODS reservists also reported economic losses in the form of additional expenses, and in many cases the additional expenses exceeded their income loss. If these additional expenses are included, approximately two-thirds of ODS mobilized reservists suffered some economic loss.

RESERVE DEMAND FOR INSURANCE

We found evidence of a fairly strong demand for mobilization insurance among reservists surveyed after ODS. We compared demand among officers and enlisted personnel at two different premium prices: $0.40 per $100 of insurance and $1.00 per $100. At the lower price, over 60 percent of officers and over 70 percent of enlisted personnel stated an interest in purchasing insurance. At the higher price, the figures fell about five percentage points for each group. The high level of demand probably reflects the need to cover income loss and additional expenses. Demand was unpredictably high among more junior personnel, for whom income losses were less frequent and more modest. However, this demand probably reflects the absence of savings or other resources to cushion any economic losses.

OPTIONS FOR STRUCTURING AND PROVIDING RESERVE INSURANCE

Policymakers would need to develop guidelines for structuring reserve insurance and we have suggested several for consideration.

- The insurance should be available to all reservists.

- Reservists should pay at least part of the costs.

- Payments should begin promptly upon mobilization.

- Purchase of insurance should occur only at preselected times outside of times of crisis.

- Reservists should chose their amounts of coverage and the need to verify economic losses should be minimized.

There are three options for providing mobilization insurance: Either the private sector or the government could act as sole insurer, or the two could share some form of partnership arrangement.

Our review of analogous types of insurance programs that share similar elements of risk suggests that private carriers alone would probably not provide coverage without large risk premiums. However, private-sector participation may be possible with limits on liabilities and risks that are spread among a large number of companies, with government participation through reinsurance for long, frequent, or very large mobilizations. We also cannot rule out the possibility of a strictly government program because of government's administrative efficiency and superior ability to estimate risks. Further analysis and discussion with insurance carriers will be required to develop specific options for insurance arrangements.

ISSUES FOR FURTHER RESEARCH

Our review of the problem suggests that economic losses are widespread and frequently large and that appropriately structured voluntary insurance coverage would probably result in significant reduction in reserve income losses. However, the feasibility of designing and implementing such a plan still requires some further work. The critical questions associated with structuring and implementing a program of income-protection insurance include:

- Should the structure of income-protection insurance be value-form or indemnity?

- How should potential adverse selection, resulting from reservists' knowledge of their mobilization chances, be handled?

- How should moral hazard arising from volunteering be handled?

- When should reservists be allowed to purchase insurance?

- What are the likely limits of private-sector coverage?

- What are the likely premiums that the private sector would charge?

- Should government be the sole insurer or reinsurer of private companies?

- What types of economic losses (business, good will, income, additional expenses) should be covered?

- What will be the tax status of insurance payments?

- Should short mobilizations and state callups be covered?

- Should reservists be charged different premiums if their callup probabilities are different?

- What will be the loss to reservists if employers discontinue pay and other benefits to reservists during times of mobilization because of insurance availability?

A key problem in designing insurance will be to address the potential moral hazard problem arising from volunteering. Volunteers in the very early part of ODS were a critical element in the early logistical movement of troops and equipment. Insurance should be designed so as not to discourage volunteering. This probably means that payments cannot depend on whether or not individuals were volunteers. However, this will introduce additional liability risk for insurers and higher premiums if volunteers' decisions are influenced by the presence of insurance coverage. Research is needed to determine the extent of volunteering, how important a role economic losses or gains played in volunteers' decisions, and how long voluntary status lasted. If volunteers were simply individuals who mobilized early because authority was not yet available, their status as volunteers might be short. On the other hand, the problem might be solved by broader early authority to call reservists.

An associated problem is whether individuals can "opt out" of involuntary callups because of economic circumstances. If personnel involuntarily called are selected on the basis of likely economic loss or gains and whether the individual purchased insurance to cover economic losses, then adverse selection will occur and insurance liability and premiums would be greater.

The tax status of insurance payments is another issue. If the benefits are tax free, then less insurance would need to be purchased; the costs to reservists would decline, but taxpayers would partially subsidize the insurance. Reservists also would not face the problem of underwithholding and having to pay large tax payments later.

Finally, one side effect of providing insurance coverage may be that private employers will not continue pay or benefits for reservists during mobilization. Approximately 20–25 percent of employers continued some form of pay for reservists during ODS, but a substantially higher number continued some form of health, pension, or other benefits. Giving reservists the opportunity to buy insurance may make employers less generous. Further research is needed on this issue also.

Any government participation in reinsurance will require legislation to implement. Should OSD policymakers decide to propose such legislation, it will be important to engage the insurance industry and the reserve community in structuring more specific options for providing coverage to best serve the different interests in the legislative process.

This report has examined the desirability and feasibility of providing income-protection insurance to reservists. We have not attempted to examine other possible solutions to the problem of income loss during mobilization. Examples of such solutions are modification of the reserve compensation system to include specific types of pay during mobilization which might be in the form of differential bonus payments to mobilized reservists. Such programs will be difficult to design if they are to meet considerations of equity and political feasibility. In addition, it will be impossible to target such programs effectively to include only those losing income. Inevitably, any targeting by occupation or paygrade will include individuals not suffering income losses, making the program somewhat inefficient. Finally, the magnitude of the bonus cannot be set to individual circumstances to cover losses, which introduces another inefficiency. The advantage of insurance appears to be that it can effectively target those losing income, and can provide variable payments that come close to matching the highly differential income losses. However, more consideration will be given to other options in a future final report.

BIBLIOGRAPHY

Besen, Stanley M., and David W. Grissmer, "Insuring Mobilized Reservists Against Economic Losses: A Preliminary Analysis," unpublished RAND research, 1992.

Coffey, Kenneth, J., "The Price They Paid: Navy Reserve Physicians and Dentists Recalled to Active Duty During the War with Iraq," mimeo., 1992.

Grissmer, David W., Richard Buddin, and Sheila Nataraj Kirby, *Improving Reserve Compensation: A Review of Current Compensation and Related Personnel and Training Readiness Issues*, RAND, R-3707-FMP/RA, September 1989.

Grissmer, David W., Sheila Nataraj Kirby, and C. Francisco, *1979 Reserve Force Studies Surveys: Weighting the Survey Data*, RAND, N-2080-RA, February 1984.

Kalton, Graham, *Compensating for Missing Survey Data*, Survey Research Center, Institute for Social Research, Research Report Series, 1983.

LaVange, Lisa M., Mary Ellen McCalla, Stuart H. Rakoff, Zahava D. Doering, Bette Mahoney, and Tim J. Gabel, *Description of Officers and Enlisted Personnel in the U.S. Selected Reserve: 1986, Supplementary Tabulations from the 1986 Reserve Components Surveys, Volume II*, Defense Manpower Data Center, Arlington, Virginia, November 1987.